DOMINANCE

2

Dominance

The Mental Game

The Psychology behind Retraining your Brain for Success and Happiness

Written by Dr. Kalesha L. Henlon

2023

Written by Dr. Kalesha L. Henlon

Published by Dr. Kalesha L. Henlon

c. 2023 by Kalhen Management Services

www.kalhencoaching.com

First Printing, 2023

Comments are welcomed.

For more information please email them to info@kalhencoaching.com

Dedicated to all the black men and women who refuse to be labelled by society standards, who strive to break away from mental slavery and continually strive for greatness – everyday.

I am so excited to write about Black Girl Magic and its importance in today's society. Black women have gone through so much, from slavery to systematic oppression, yet we have continued to thrive and rise above it all. We have created our own lane in the world and showed up and showed out every time. The term "Black Girl Magic" has been coined to celebrate the strength, beauty, and power of black women and girls.

Let's talk about the significance of dedicating yourself to Black Girl Magic and how it can change the game for us as individuals and as a community.

The First Step: Self Love

The first step to dedicating yourself to Black Girl Magic is to start with self-love. As black women, we are often subjected to societal beauty standards that do not necessarily cater to our unique features. It is important to remember that we are beautiful, powerful, and capable of doing anything we set our minds to. So, take the time to love yourself, embrace your unique beauty, and celebrate your individuality. Once you start with self-love, the magic will follow.

The Second Step: Support Other Black Women

As the popular saying goes, "there is power in numbers." The same goes for the magic of Black Girl Magic. Supporting and uplifting other black women and girls is crucial in our journey to excellence. This can be as simple as a compliment, a word of encouragement, or even sharing and promoting their work. When we come together and support one another, we can break down barriers and create a stronger, more united community.

The Third Step: Embrace Your Culture

The beauty of Black Girl Magic lies in our culture and heritage. Our traditions, style, and overall essence have been the blueprint for many things today. Embrace your culture, learn about your history, and celebrate it every chance you get. Whether it's through music, art, food, or fashion, take pride in where you come from and let it reflect in everything you do.

The Fourth Step: Expand Your Knowledge

Knowledge is power, and the more knowledge we have about ourselves and our place in the world, the more powerful we become. Take the time to read books, watch documentaries, attend lectures, and engage in meaningful conversations about issues that affect black women and girls. Through expanding your knowledge, you can become better equipped to navigate the world and create change in your community.

The Fifth Step: Take Action

Dedicating yourself to Black Girl Magic is not just about talking the talk, it's about walking the walk. Take action in your community, whether it's volunteering, advocating for change, or starting your own project. Use your voice and your talents to make a difference. The more we take action, the more we can change the world.

Dedicating yourself to Black Girl Magic is not just a movement, it's a way of life. It's about celebrating and embracing who we are as black women while uplifting and empowering others. Through self-love, support, culture, knowledge, and action, we can create magic and make a positive impact on our world.

So, let's go out there and continue to shine like the queens we are.

Black Girl Magic forever!

8

In my first book, Eradicating Limiting Beliefs – Becoming the Boss of Your Circumstances, I spoke about the importance of mindset. How, when we actively retrain our brain, we can achieve anything in life. If I wanted it, I went after it.

Breaking the Inferior Mindset: Embracing Black Girl Magic

When it comes to being a black girl in contemporary society, countless challenges and obstacles inevitably come to mind. However, one of the toughest struggles is the inferior mindset that is all too prevalent in our communities, one which makes many of us feel like we're constantly coming up short and not measuring up. This limiting belief system has been instilled in black women for generations, and it's time to put an end to it. Through the magic of resilience, perseverance, and self-acceptance, we can break free of this mental trap and embrace black girl magic to live our best lives.

How do we achieve this?

Recognizing the Inferior Mindset: Before we can break free of limiting beliefs, we first need to be aware of them. Many black women grow up with the notion that they are inferior to others, based on factors like skin color, hair texture, and body type. Society perpetuates this harmful narrative by promoting Eurocentric beauty standards and shaming those who fall outside of them. Additionally, we often hear harmful messages from our own families or peers, suggesting that we aren't pretty or smart enough. It's time to recognize that these beliefs do not define us.

Overcoming Stereotypes and Misconceptions: Another layer of the inferior mindset stems from the stereotypes and misconceptions that are placed on black women. For example, we may be seen as "angry" or "aggressive" simply for speaking out about injustice or advocating for our rights. Alternatively, we may be fetishized and objectified by those who see us only as sexual objects. To counter these harmful narratives, we need to challenge them head-on and make our voices heard.

Celebrating Black Girl Magic: At the core of breaking free from the inferior mindset is embracing black girl magic – that is, celebrating all of the unique qualities that make us who we are. Whether it's our natural hair, our curves, or our intelligence and strength, these attributes are part of our beauty and power. Beyond just celebrating ourselves, we can uplift and support other black women as well, recognizing that our collective magic is stronger than any negative beliefs that try to hold us back.

Activating Change through Self-Love: While it's important to recognize the challenges that black women face, it's equally crucial to focus on self-love and care. By taking ownership of our worth and value, we can start to shift the narrative and make way for positive change. When we love ourselves, we are better able to stand up for ourselves and demand the respect and rights that we deserve.

Keeping the Magic Alive: Finally, we must continue to promote and reinforce the concept of black girl magic for future generations. By teaching young black girls to love and embrace themselves, we can create a ripple effect of positivity and self-acceptance. This means sharing our stories, being visible and vocal in our communities, and supporting organizations that uplift and empower black women and girls.

Breaking free of the inferior mindset is an ongoing journey that requires patience, resilience, and a whole lot of self-love. But when we tap into our black girl magic, we can move mountains and break down barriers. By recognizing and counteracting harmful narratives, celebrating our unique qualities, and promoting self-love and activism, we can create a brighter future for all black women. So, let's keep the magic alive, and let our brilliance shine!

Dr. Kal

Dr. Kalesha L. Henlon

Yamanashi, Japan

May 27, 2023

12

The Happiest Brain: The Psychology of Retraining Your Brain for Success and Happiness

Our brains are amazing machines that are constantly adapting to the world around us. Unfortunately, our brains aren't always wired for happiness and success. Stress, anxiety, and negative thinking can take hold and make it difficult for us to achieve our goals. The good news is that we can retrain our brains to think positively and achieve our wildest dreams.

In this book, we will explore the psychology of retraining your brain for success and happiness.

What is the Psychology of Retraining Your Brain?

The psychology of retraining your brain is based on the idea of neuroplasticity, which explains how our brains are capable of changing and adapting throughout our lives. Neuroscientists have discovered that we can change our brain's neural pathways by changing our thoughts and behaviors. The idea is to replace negative, self-limiting beliefs with positive, empowering ones. This retraining process involves a lot of conscious effort and repetition to promote the formation of new neural connections.

The Benefits of Positive Thinking

Positive thinking has long been associated with better mental health, lower stress levels, and improved overall well-being. By thinking positively, we train our brains to approach situations with a growth mindset instead of a fixed mindset. This means that we see setbacks as learning opportunities rather than failures. A positive mindset also helps us to overcome obstacles and achieve our goals with more ease and grace.

The Power of Affirmations

Affirmations are positive statements that we repeat to ourselves regularly. They can help replace negative self-talk with positive, empowering language. Some popular affirmations include "I am worthy of success" and "I am capable of achieving my dreams." By repeating affirmations regularly, we can train our brains to believe these positive statements, which can help us achieve success and happiness.

Building Positive Habits

Our habits play a huge role in shaping our thoughts and behavior. By building positive habits like meditation, exercise, and journaling, we can retrain our brains to think positively. These habits can help us manage stress, anxiety, and negative self-talk more effectively, leading to better mental health and overall happiness.

Building a Supportive Community

We are social creatures, and our connections to others play a critical role in our well-being. Building a supportive community of friends, family, and mentors can help us stay motivated and on track and provide us with the encouragement and support we need to succeed.

Retraining your brain for success and happiness is a lifelong process that requires effort and dedication. By adopting positive habits, practicing mindfulness, and building supportive relationships, we can lay the foundation for a happier, more fulfilling life. Remember, your thoughts shape your reality, so choose carefully and think positively!

A Guide to Dominating Your Mind

Learning to dominate your mind is both exciting and overwhelming. The pressure to succeed academically and socially can often lead to stress, anxiety, and other mental health issues. However, with the right mindset and approach, you can overcome these challenges and dominate your mind.

Here are some tips and strategies to help you take control of your thoughts and emotions and achieve success and happiness, internally and externally.

Practice mindfulness meditation

Mindfulness meditation refers to the practice of paying attention to the present moment without judgment. It has been shown to reduce stress, increase focus and concentration, and improve overall well-being. Whether you are new to meditation or have been practicing for some time, incorporating mindfulness into your daily routine can have significant benefits for your mental and emotional health. Set aside a few minutes each day to sit quietly, breathe deeply, and focus on your thoughts and feelings. With practice, you will develop greater awareness and control over your mind, allowing you to navigate even the most challenging situations with ease.

Develop a growth mindset

A growth mindset is the belief that your abilities and traits can be developed and improved through hard work and dedication. In contrast, a fixed mindset is the belief that your abilities and traits are predetermined and cannot be changed. By adopting a growth mindset, you will be better equipped to handle setbacks and failures, as you will see them as opportunities for growth and learning rather than as indications of your limitations. This mindset can also help you cultivate a sense of purpose and motivation, as you work towards achieving your goals with a sense of optimism and resilience.

Set realistic and achievable goals

Setting goals is an essential step in achieving success, but it's essential to make them realistic and achievable. Many people set unrealistic expectations for themselves, leading to disappointment and a sense of failure. Instead, break down your goals into smaller, more manageable steps, and focus on making progress rather than achieving perfection. Celebrate your successes along the way, and don't be too hard on yourself when things don't go according to plan. Remember that setbacks are a natural part of the learning process, and that every mistake is an opportunity to grow and learn.

Surround yourself with positive and supportive people

The people you surround yourself with can have a big impact on your mental and emotional health. Seek out friends and mentors who are positive, supportive, and share your goals and values. These people can provide you with encouragement, guidance, and a sense of community, making it easier to cope with the inevitable ups and downs of life. Conversely, avoid people who are negative, critical, or unsupportive, as they can drain your energy and make it harder to stay focused and motivated.

Take care of your physical health

Finally, don't forget about the importance of physical health in maintaining a strong and resilient mind. Get enough sleep, eat a healthy and balanced diet, and engage in regular exercise. These habits can help reduce stress, boost your immunity, and improve your mood and energy levels. Additionally, practicing self-care activities such as yoga, massage, or journaling can provide you with a sense of calm and relaxation that can help you cope with the demands of life.

Life can be challenging and stressful, but with the right mindset and approach, you can overcome these challenges and achieve success both academically and personally. By practicing mindfulness meditation, developing a growth mindset, setting realistic goals, surrounding yourself with positive people, and taking care of your physical health, you can take control of your thoughts and emotions and dominate your mind. Remember that progress, not perfection, is the goal, and that every step you take towards achieving your goals is a step in the right direction.

Contents

19

Chapter 1
Black Girl Magic

Black Girl Magic is about embracing and celebrating the achievements of African-American women despite all odds. It is a term that was coined to remind us that black women are capable of overcoming historical oppression, rising above prejudices, and succeeding in areas such as business and education. Black Girl Magic is also an encouragement for young black girls to stay focused on their dreams no matter what obstacles they may face. It is an empowering phrase that serves to remind us that despite the odds, black women can still achieve greatness. Black Girl Magic is about showing the world what amazing things black women are capable of when given the opportunity and support. It is a reminder that we have a responsibility to continue uplifting each other and supporting one another in our endeavors. So, let's celebrate our Black Girl Magic and continue to rise above the odds.

Black Girl Magic isn't just a buzzword - it's a reminder of the strength, resilience and power of black women everywhere. By celebrating Black Girl Magic, we honor generations of powerful women who have blazed trails in their communities and fought against all odds to make a difference. Whether it's creating art that celebrates our unique beauty, or advocating for social justice and racial equality, black women have been at the forefront of progress in many ways. Unfortunately, too often we are still afraid to fully embrace the greatness of being black – Black Girl Magic is here to remind us that our differences should be celebrated. No matter what you look like, where you come from, or what your background may be, you can create your own special brand of magic! So don't be afraid – let Black Girl Magic inspire you to reach heights you never thought possible. Go on and show the world what you got!

It's time to break the mold and embrace all that makes us unique. Black Girl Magic is here to remind us of our power, our potential, and our beauty, so go ahead - show the world what you got!

Be bold. Be fearless. Be unapologetically black! With Black Girl Magic in your corner, anything is possible. And remember, it's not just about facing the challenge that lies ahead - it's also about appreciating the journey and embracing your differences. Let Black Girl Magic lighten your load and be sure to always shine your bright, beautiful light!

Let's keep the spirit of Black Girl Magic alive and show the world what it means to be a brave, powerful black woman. From everyday acts of resilience to major social movements, let's continue to create change and make our mark on history. It's time to shine!

No matter what obstacles you face, with a little bit of Black Girl Magic in your corner, you can achieve anything. So never be afraid to go against the grain and take on whatever challenges come your way; We got this! Together we can keep empowering and inspiring one another to be our best selves and make our dreams come true.

Black Girl Magic is here to support, inspire, and remind us that anything is possible! So don't be afraid - this is your time to shine! Celebrate your differences, embrace your power, and never stop creating. Let's keep pushing ourselves to reach new heights and continue our mission of empowerment and resilience.

Let your Black Girl Magic blaze the trail! The world is ready for all that you have to offer, so go ahead and show them what you got! Together we can create a brighter future and break down all barriers in our paths. Be the light that inspires others to reach for their dreams, and never forget the power of Black Girl Magic!

No matter what the future holds, Black Girl Magic will always be here to help us believe in ourselves and keep striving for greatness. So go forth fearlessly, never give up, and let your light shine bright!

So, are you ready to unleash your Black Girl Magic? Let's get out there and make our mark on the world! Don't be afraid of being black - it is an amazing privilege that we have been blessed with. There is no limit to what you can achieve when you believe in yourself, and that is what Black Girl Magic is all about. Go forth and conquer!

Remember: Nothing can stop you from pursuing your goals - not even your greatest fears. With Black Girl Magic in your corner, you can do anything. So go ahead and believe in yourself; We've got your back!

Black girls are magic, and there's no denying that. From our stunning natural hair to our undeniable creativity, we've always been a force to be reckoned with. But what is Black girl magic, and why is it so important to embrace it? Black girl magic is the idea that Black women are inherently magical, talented, and beautiful, regardless of their skin tone, hair texture, or body shape. Today, we're going to talk about why Black girl magic matters, how to embrace it, and why it's essential to tap into this inner magic at an early age.

Reasons to Embrace your Black Girl Magic

Black girl magic is a form of self-love

Historically, Black women have been subjected to racism, sexism, and discrimination, which can take a toll on our self-esteem. Black girl magic is a form of self-love that allows us to celebrate our unique and extraordinary qualities. When we embrace our natural hair, love our melanin-rich skin, and showcase our creativity, we're saying to the world that Black women are phenomenal and worthy of admiration.

Black girl magic is a symbol of collective power

When we celebrate Black women's achievements, we're not only uplifting individuals, but we're also building community power. Black girl magic is a reminder to our sisters that we're in this together, and when one of us wins, we all win. It's a way to cultivate sisterhood and create a sense of belonging in a world that often seeks to divide us.

Black girl magic is a resistance to stereotypes

Contrary to negative stereotypes about us, Black women are doctors, lawyers, business owners, artists, and educators. We're smart, innovative, and capable of phenomenal things. When we embrace and showcase our Black girl magic, we're debunking harmful stereotypes perpetuated about Black women and creating new narratives about who we are and what we can achieve.

How to Embrace Your Black Girl Magic

Embracing your Black girl magic doesn't mean you have to be perfect or know everything. Instead, it's about amplifying your unique skills, talents, and interests. For example, if you're a writer, write stories that reflect the experiences of Black women and girls. If you're good at doing hair, offer to help style a friend's wig or natural hair. If you're an artist, create pieces that showcase the beauty and complexity of Black women.

Why Embracing Your Black Girl Magic is Essential for Growth

Life can be challenging for anyone. Still, it can be even more challenging for Black women, who face unique hurdles such as microaggressions, lack of representation, and imposter syndrome. Embracing your Black girl magic can provide a beacon of hope during these challenging times. It can also help you connect with other Black women in society, find mentors, and create a sense of belonging.

In summary, Black girl magic is a powerful movement that celebrates the beauty, strength, and creativity of Black women. Embracing your Black girl magic can improve your self-esteem, build community power, resist stereotypes, and provide hope during challenging times. So, to all the Black women out there, keep shining your light, embrace your unique and extraordinary qualities, and remember that you're magic!

26

As a college student with darker skin, I always felt self-conscious about my appearance. Growing up, I was often teased for my complexion and I remember wishing that I could just blend in with my peers. The fear of being judged and discriminated against because of my black skin held me back and made me doubt myself. However, as I've grown older and learned to embrace my identity, I've come to realize that being a person of color is something to be proud of.

Sounds familiar?

Let's explore how to overcome the fear and self-doubt and how you too can learn to love your black skin.

Confronting Negative Beauty Standards:

As a society, we're constantly bombarded with images of beauty that prioritize people with lighter skin. Growing up, we internalized these standards and believed that we could never be considered beautiful because of our darker complexion. However, as we start to consume more media that celebrated diversity and representation, we can challenge these negative ideas. Started following black models and influencers on social media and see how they embraced their skin color and celebrated their unique features.

Surrounding yourself with positive messages of self-love can help combat the harmful effects of negative beauty standards.

Learning about Black History and Culture:

Another way I found empowerment in my black identity was by learning about the history and culture of people of color. In school, we're often taught about white European history, which can reinforce a sense of otherness for students of color. However, there's a rich and diverse history of black people throughout the world that's worth exploring. Whether it's reading about prominent black figures in history or discovering different styles of black art and music, educating yourself about black culture can help you feel more connected to your heritage.

Community and Support:

Finding a community of people who share your experiences and identity can be incredibly affirming. As a college student, I sought out black student organizations and events, which provided a space for me to connect with others and share my thoughts and feelings. Having a supportive network can be especially helpful when you're feeling discouraged or alone. It's important to seek out people who uplift you and encourage you to be proud of who you are.

Self-Care and Self-Love:

Taking care of yourself both physically and mentally is crucial to feeling confident and comfortable in your skin. This can include things like getting enough sleep, eating nutritious food, and practicing self-compassion. When you learn to love and care for yourself, you'll feel more empowered to embrace your blackness. Self-care looks different for everyone, so it's important to find what works for you and prioritize it as much as you can.

Advocating for Change:

Finally, it's important to take action and advocate for change when you see discrimination and bias happening around you. Whether it's signing petitions, speaking out against microaggressions, or demanding policy changes at your school or workplace, standing up for your rights and the rights of others is an important way to show pride in your blackness. It's not always easy, but it's necessary to create a more equitable world.

Embracing your black skin and identity can be a challenging journey, but it's also incredibly rewarding. As you work on dismantling negative beauty standards, learning about black history and culture, finding support in your community, practicing self-care and advocating for change, you'll discover a newfound sense of confidence and pride in your identity. The key is to take it one step at a time and remember that you're not alone. Together, we can create a world where everyone is celebrated for their unique backgrounds and experiences.

As a Black woman, and a lover of all things magic, I have been captivated by the concept of Black girl magic. The term has become increasingly popular in recent years and has taken on a life of its own, especially on social media. But what exactly is Black girl magic, and why is it important for us to embrace it? We will explore the power of Black girl magic as a form of self-love and how it can positively impact our lives.

What is Black girl magic?

Black girl magic is the celebration of the beauty, resilience, and excellence of Black women and girls. It is the recognition of our unique experiences, our cultural contributions, and our individuality. It is the acknowledgment of our strength in the face of adversities such as racism, sexism, and more. Black girl magic is a movement that highlights the inherent magic that exists within us and encourages us to love and appreciate ourselves and each other.

Why is it important to embrace Black girl magic?

Embracing Black girl magic means embracing ourselves in our full glory. It means recognizing and celebrating all that makes us who we are, including our history, culture, talents, and individual journeys. It means owning our beauty and intelligence, our strength and vulnerability, our flaws and our perfections. When we embrace Black girl magic, we are not only loving ourselves, but we're empowering and uplifting other Black women and girls. We are reminding ourselves and the world that Black women and girls are magical, valuable, and deserving of respect and recognition.

How can Black girl magic promote self-love?

Black girl magic can promote self-love by providing us with a positive, affirming lens through which to view ourselves. It challenges us to embrace ourselves in our entirety, flaws and all, and not try to conform to society's narrow standards of beauty and success. It encourages us to actively seek out and celebrate the beauty and achievements of other Black women and girls, which in turn reinforces our own worth and value. When we internalize the message of Black girl magic, we become more confident, more resilient, and more self-loving.

What are some ways to cultivate Black girl magic in our lives?

There are many ways to cultivate Black girl magic in our lives, such as:

1. Celebrating our heritage: Learning about and embracing our cultural heritage is an important aspect of Black girl magic. This can include exploring our family history, learning about our ancestral traditions and practices, and engaging with Black cultural expressions such as music, art, literature, and more.

2. Connecting with other Black women and girls: Building relationships with other Black women and girls can be a powerful source of strength and support. Whether through social media, mentorship programs, or community organizations, connecting with other Black women and girls can help us feel seen, heard, and validated.

3. Prioritizing self-care: Practicing self-care is essential for cultivating Black girl magic. This can include activities such as meditation, exercise, journaling, and spending time doing things we love. Taking care of our physical, emotional, and spiritual well-being is a way of showing love and respect to ourselves.

Black girl magic is a celebration of the inherent magic that exists within Black women and girls. Embracing Black girl magic means loving and celebrating ourselves in our entirety, and empowering and uplifting other Black women and girls. The power of Black girl magic lies in its ability to promote self-love and confidence, and to challenge the narrow standards of beauty and success that society imposes on us. By cultivating Black girl magic in our lives, we can create a more positive, affirming, and empowering world for ourselves and each other.

Black Girl Magic is a term that has come to represent the beauty, power, resilience, and strength of black women around the world. It celebrates all that black women have achieved, despite having to overcome slavery and the mentalities that come with it. Through Black Girl Magic, black women are rising above the odds to become successful in their fields and show the world just how powerful they can be. It's all about recognizing the unique gifts and talents of women of color, while also empowering each other to reach higher goals. By connecting across various disciplines—from business to arts and entertainment to health—black women are becoming the change makers that they know they can be. Whether it's through mentorship, entrepreneurship, or simply having a platform for creativity and self-expression—Black Girl Magic is about claiming our power and using it to make our world a better place. So, if you're a black woman looking to take your power back, take inspiration from Black Girl Magic and don't be afraid to embrace your own power. You can do it!

Black Girl Magic is a movement that celebrates the triumphs, resilience, and success of black women. It is an acknowledgment of the collective power of black women and a reminder to them that anything is possible. From overcoming slavery mentality to rising above the odds, Black Girl Magic celebrates the achievements of black women in all walks of life.

Black Girl Magic encourages us to embrace our power as successful, strong, and independent black women. We can push ourselves forward by recognizing our unique strengths, talents, and accomplishments. We can break away from traditional notions of gender roles and stand tall as successful black women.

Black Girl Magic is a reminder to the world that we are capable of achieving greatness despite any odds that may be stacked against us. It is a call for other black women to recognize their own greatness and join us in creating an even brighter future.

In order to truly celebrate Black Girl Magic, we must continue to support and uplift each other. We can do this by using our platforms to create more visibility for black women in all industries, from the arts to finance. We can also create safe spaces where black women have the opportunity to network and collaborate with one another. By creating these opportunities, we can celebrate Black Girl Magic and continue to rise above the odds.

So, don't be afraid to let your light shine! You are a powerful black woman and you have the power to make a difference in this world. Be proud of who you are, embrace your talents, and claim your rightful place in the universe as an amazing example of Black Girl Magic!

By allowing our collective voices to be heard, we can continue to celebrate the success of black women everywhere. Let's keep spreading the message and showing that Black Girl Magic is real and it is here to stay!

Thanks for joining us in this celebration!

Together, we are unstoppable.

Let's keep it going!

Chapter 2

Eradicating Slavery Mentality

This topic has been around since the dawn of civilization: slavery. While for many of us, the idea of actual physical enslavement seems like a distant concept, this mentality of being imprisoned by our own thoughts, habits, and societal norms is still all too prevalent.

My goal is to dive into what slavery mentality is, how it impacts us, and what we can do to eradicate it from our lives once and for all. So, buckle up and hold on tight - we're in for a wild ride.

First off, what exactly is slavery mentality? It's not just about chains and whips. Slavery mentality is the idea that people are not able to control their own circumstances and are at the mercy of external factors, which is a limiting belief. This can take many forms, from thinking you'll never be able to achieve your dreams because of your background, to feeling like you're stuck in a dead-end job because that's all you're good at.

The impact of this mentality can be devastating. Mental slavery keeps us stagnant, increasing feelings of hopelessness and despair and leading to something called learned helplessness. This is when individuals become conditioned into the belief that they are powerless in the face of their circumstances, making them more likely to give up when faced with obstacles and less likely to take meaningful action to effect change in their lives.

How can we break free from the chains of mental slavery? A good starting point is to recognize when we're exhibiting signs of learned helplessness. This includes feelings of powerlessness, hopelessness, and apathy about our own lives. Once we've identified this pattern in ourselves, we can start to shift our mindset towards one of empowerment.

This means taking active steps towards our goals, rather than waiting for things to happen to us. It also means recognizing that we are not defined by our past or our circumstances, and that we have the power to change our lives for the better. This requires breaking free from societal norms and expectations, and instead forging our own path towards a life of authenticity and fulfilment.

Another way to eradicate slavery mentality is by challenging the narrative around perfection. We live in a society that glorifies the idea of being perfect. But the truth is, perfectionism is often just a mask for fear of failure or rejection, leading to procrastination and avoidance.

We need to embrace the idea of progress over perfection, recognizing that the journey towards our goals is often messy and imperfect. Instead of focusing solely on the end result, we should celebrate small wins along the way, recognizing that each step brings us closer to our ultimate destination.

Ultimately, breaking free from slavery mentality requires recognizing that we are in control of our lives, and that our circumstances do not define us. It requires a willingness to challenge the status quo and forge our own paths, prioritizing growth and progress over perfection.

But it's important to remember that this is not a one-and-done process. Eradicating slavery mentality is an ongoing journey, one that requires a commitment to personal growth and development.

The slavery mentality is a pervasive and destructive force that restricts our ability to live fulfilling lives. But by recognizing the patterns of learned helplessness within ourselves and taking active steps towards empowerment, we can break free from these mental chains and embrace the freedom to grow, learn, and thrive. Remember, no matter how long you've been trapped in mental slavery, it's never too late to take the first step towards a life of authenticity, fulfilment, and freedom.

Chapter 3
Eradicating Limiting Beliefs

Limiting beliefs can shackle us and keep us from achieving our goals, dreams, and aspirations. These beliefs are often deeply ingrained in our subconscious minds, and we aren't always aware of their negative impact on our lives. However, with a little introspection and a strong desire for personal growth, we can overcome limiting beliefs and achieve anything we set our minds to.

Everyone struggles with self-doubt, fear of failure, and negative self-talk. It's time to take charge of your thoughts and transform your mindset. We'll explore the power of positive thinking and provide practical strategies for eradicating limiting beliefs.

1. Identify your limiting beliefs

The first step in overcoming limiting beliefs is identifying what they are. These beliefs can show up in different areas of your life, such as your finances, relationships, or career. Ask yourself, "What do I believe about myself that is holding me back?" Write down these beliefs and challenge their validity. Are they really true, or are they just a product of your imagination?

2. Create a new belief system

Once you've identified your limiting beliefs, it's time to create a new belief system. Instead of focusing on what you can't do, focus on what you can do. Replace negative self-talk with positive affirmations. Write down these affirmations and repeat them daily. For example, if you believe you're not good enough to apply for a particular job, replace that belief with "I am capable and deserving of this opportunity."

3. Take action

Positive thinking alone won't make your dreams a reality. You need to take action to overcome your limiting beliefs. Start by setting small goals that align with your new belief system. Celebrate your successes, no matter how small they may seem. As you achieve your goals, your confidence will grow, and your limiting beliefs will fade away.

4. Surround yourself with positivity

The company you keep can have a significant impact on your mindset. Surround yourself with positive, supportive individuals who believe in you and your potential. Join clubs or organizations that align with your interests and goals. Attend workshops or seminars that focus on personal growth and development.

5. Embrace failure

Failure is an essential part of personal growth. Don't let fear of failure hold you back from taking risks and pursuing your dreams. Instead, embrace failure as an opportunity to learn and grow. Reflect on your experiences, identify what went wrong, and make changes. Remember, failure is not a reflection of your worth or value as a person.

Eradicating limiting beliefs takes time, effort, and a willingness to embrace change. But the rewards are well worth it. By changing how you think and feel about yourself, you can achieve your goals, conquer your fears, and become the best version of yourself. Remember, you are not defined by your past beliefs or experiences. With a positive, growth-oriented mindset, anything is possible. Start today by identifying your limiting beliefs, creating a new belief system, taking action, surrounding yourself with positivity, and embracing failure. You've got this!

Chapter 4
Dominating Life

College life can be overwhelming, stressful and downright chaotic. As a student, you have to juggle attending classes, studying, maintaining a social life, and preparing for your future. It can be extremely challenging, but with the right mindset and strategies, you can dominate your life in college and beyond. Here are useful strategies that will help you take control of your life and achieve success in all aspects.

Create a Schedule:

One of the best ways to dominate your life is by creating a schedule that works for you. Start by getting a planner or using an app to organize your time. Set specific goals for the day, week, and month. Make sure to include time for studying, attending classes, exercising, and socializing. Remember to be realistic with your goals and don't overextend yourself, or you'll end up feeling overwhelmed.

Focus on Time Management:

Time management is key to dominating your life in college and beyond. Prioritize your tasks, and break them down into smaller, more manageable parts. Use time management techniques to increase your productivity. Be dedicated to your studies and make sure to take advantage of all the resources available to you, such as tutoring, office hours, study groups, and online resources.

Maintain a Healthy Lifestyle:

To dominate your life, you have to take care of your body and mind. Make sure to eat healthy, exercise regularly, and get enough sleep. Avoid unhealthy habits such as excessive drinking, unhealthy eating, and procrastination. Take care of your mental health by practicing self-care regularly- whether it's by meditating or seeking professional help. A healthy lifestyle may seem unimportant, but it's essential to creating a healthy and successful future.

Stay Motivated:

Staying motivated can be challenging, especially when things seem tough. Find your purpose and motivation in life and create a vision board or motivational quotes that inspire you. Set achievable goals and celebrate your accomplishments - no matter how small they may be. Surround yourself with positive and supportive people that motivate you and find ways to reward yourself when you achieve your goals. Remember, motivation is key to dominating your life.

Embrace Change:

Life is unpredictable, and change is inevitable. To dominate your life, you have to learn to embrace change and adapt to new situations. Don't be afraid to step out of your comfort zone and try new things. Take risks, make mistakes, learn, and grow. Remember that every failure is a lesson learned, and every setback is an opportunity to move forward. Embrace change, and you'll see your life transform for the better.

Dominating your life in college and beyond is all about having the right mindset, planning, prioritizing, and being dedicated to your goals. By creating a schedule, focusing on time management, maintaining a healthy lifestyle, staying motivated, and embracing change, you can take control of your life and achieve success in all aspects. Remember that dominating your life is not a one-time deal but a continuous process that requires effort, patience, and perseverance. Start taking action today and watch your life transform for the better.

Chapter 5

Dominating Relationships

Relationships are a delicate dance between two people. It involves trust, respect, and a willingness to compromise. However, there are times when one person may feel that they need to take control and dominate the relationship. While dominance may seem like a dirty word, it doesn't have to be. In fact, when done right, dominating your relationship can actually be healthy and beneficial for both partners.

But before we dive into the details of dominating your relationship, let's be clear about what we mean by dominance. Domination does not mean being overbearing, abusive, or controlling. It means taking charge of the relationship in a positive and constructive way. It means being confident, assertive, and proactive.

If you're ready to take your relationship to the next level, here are some tips on how to dominate your relationship (without being overbearing).

Set the tone

The first step in dominating your relationship is to set the tone. You need to establish yourself as the leader in the relationship. This means being confident and decisive in your actions and decisions. It also means communicating your expectations clearly and setting boundaries.

For example, if you want your partner to be more attentive to your needs, don't be afraid to ask for what you want. Be firm but fair, and make it clear that you expect them to follow through. By setting the tone, you create a sense of order and direction in your relationship, and your partner will be more likely to follow your lead.

Take charge

Once you have set the tone, it's time to take charge. This means being proactive and taking action to make your relationship better. Identify areas that need improvement and come up with a plan of action to address them. This could be anything from scheduling more date nights to initiating more physical contact.

When you take charge, you show your partner that you are committed to making your relationship work. It also demonstrates your willingness to take the lead and make tough decisions. But remember, taking charge doesn't mean being bossy or controlling. It means being a strong and decisive partner.

Be assertive

Being assertive is an important part of dominating your relationship. It means being able to express your needs and wants in a clear and confident manner. This can be tough for some people, especially if you're used to keeping quiet or avoiding conflict. But the key to being assertive is to communicate with respect and empathy.

For example, if your partner does something that bothers you, don't just let it slide. Instead, calmly express your feelings and explain why it bothers you. Use "I" statements instead of "you" statements to avoid sounding accusatory. By being assertive, you show your partner that you have a voice in the relationship.

Be confident

Confidence is key when it comes to dominating your relationship. It means believing in yourself and your abilities as a partner. But confidence can be tricky, especially if you have insecurities or doubts about yourself. The key is to focus on your strengths and not be afraid to show them off.

For example, if you know you're great in bed, don't be shy about taking charge in the bedroom. Or if you're a fantastic cook, show off your skills by planning a romantic dinner for two. By being confident in your abilities, you show your partner that you are a strong and capable partner.

Support your partner

Dominating your relationship doesn't mean that you ignore your partner's needs and wants. It's important to support your partner and make them feel valued and appreciated. This means listening to their concerns, being attentive to their needs, and showing them love and affection.

Remember, a strong and healthy relationship is built on mutual respect and trust. Dominating your relationship can be a positive and effective way to strengthen these bonds and bring you and your partner closer together.

Dominating your relationship doesn't have to be a scary or negative thing. When done right, it can be a healthy and beneficial way to improve your relationship and bring you and your partner closer together. By setting the tone, taking charge, being assertive, being confident, and supporting your partner, you can establish yourself as a leader in your relationship without being overbearing or controlling. So go ahead, take the lead, and dominate your relationship in the best way possible.

Chapter 6
Fixed Mindset VS Growth Mindset

Have you ever been told that you're not smart enough or talented enough to achieve your dreams? Or have you ever thought that some people are just born with natural abilities and there's nothing you can do to improve yourself? If you answered yes, then you might have a fixed mindset.

A fixed mindset is a belief system where individuals believe that their intelligence, talents, and abilities are fixed and cannot be improved. This mindset is limiting because it can prevent people from trying new things and taking risks. Let's explore the concept of fixed mindset, how it affects us and what can be done to change it.

Understanding the Fixed Mindset

A fixed mindset can be traced back to Carol Dweck, a Stanford University psychologist who conducted extensive research on the topic. According to Dweck, people with a fixed mindset believe that their qualities are set in stone and they tend to avoid challenges, give up easily, and feel threatened by the success of others.

Effects of Fixed Mindset on College and University Students

College and university students who have a fixed mindset may feel discouraged if they receive a poor grade on an assignment or an exam and may believe that they're not smart enough to succeed. Similarly, if they struggle with a particular subject, they may give up on it altogether instead of putting in the effort to improve.

Developing a Growth Mindset

The good news is, it's possible to shift from a fixed mindset to a growth mindset. Developing a growth mindset involves recognizing that your abilities can be improved through effort and persistence. Here are some strategies that can help:

- Embrace challenges: instead of avoiding them, seek out challenges that will help you grow and learn.
- Learn from failure: failure is not a reflection of your abilities, but rather an opportunity to learn and improve.
- Believe in the power of effort: put in the time and effort to improve yourself, and don't give up when faced with obstacles.
- Practice self-compassion: be kind to yourself and recognize that everyone makes mistakes and has weaknesses.

Benefits of a Growth Mindset

Having a growth mindset can lead to a number of benefits, including:

- Increased motivation and persistence
- Improved resilience in the face of challenges
- Greater creativity and problem-solving abilities
- Greater willingness to learn and try new things

Having a fixed mindset can be limiting, but it's not permanent. By recognizing and challenging our fixed mindset beliefs, we can shift towards a growth mindset and unlock our full potential. This involves embracing challenges, persevering through failure, and believing in our own ability to improve. As college and university students, you are constantly faced with new challenges and opportunities for growth. By adopting a growth mindset, you can make the most of these opportunities and achieve our goals.

Have you ever been told you're just not good at something? Or that you'll never be able to achieve your goals? If so, you've probably found yourself with a fixed mindset - the belief that your abilities and intelligence are set in stone and can't be changed much. But what if we told you that you could actually change your mindset and transform your approach to learning and achieving your goals? That's what a growth mindset is all about. Here's why you need one to succeed in college and beyond.

A Growth Mindset Allows You to Embrace Challenges

In a fixed mindset, challenges are seen as threats to your intelligence or talent. This can make you avoid new or difficult tasks, fearing failure and likely setting you up for setbacks down the road. But with a growth mindset, challenges are viewed as opportunities to learn and grow. You recognize that failure and struggle are necessary for progress, so you're more likely to push through and persist in the face of difficulty.

You'll Train Your Brain for Lifelong Learning

When you believe that you can learn and improve, your brain is more open to taking in new information and exploring different methods of problem-solving. With a growth mindset, you're not limited by what you already know - you seek out new information to expand your knowledge and skills. This adaptability will serve you well not only in college but in any career or personal pursuit you take on.

Failure and Feedback Aren't Personal Attacks

A fixed mindset can make it difficult to receive feedback or accept failure. When your abilities are seen as absolute and unchanging, any criticism or misstep can feel like a commentary on you as a person. But a growth mindset allows you to detach your sense of self-worth from your abilities. Failure is viewed as a learning opportunity, and feedback is welcomed as a way to improve and grow.

You'll Be More Resilient to Setbacks

No one goes through college or life without encountering setbacks, disappointments, or even failures. But with a growth mindset, these setbacks are seen as temporary and not reflective of your abilities or potential. You recognize that success is not a linear path but a journey with ups and downs. This resilience will help you bounce back from disappointment and keep pushing towards your goals.

You'll Have a More Positive Outlook on Life

A growth mindset can also improve your overall outlook on life. When you have a sense of personal agency and believe that you can improve, you're more likely to approach new situations with confidence and a can-do attitude. This optimism can help you stay motivated in the face of challenges and bounce back from setbacks more quickly. Plus, it just feels good to know that you have the power to shape your future.

A growth mindset isn't something that everyone is born with - it's a mindset that's developed over time with practice and intentional effort. By cultivating this attitude, you can transform your approach to learning and achieving your goals, both in college and beyond. Embracing challenges, seeking out new information, viewing failure as an opportunity for growth, being resilient to setbacks, and maintaining a positive outlook are all key elements of a growth mindset that can serve you well throughout your life. With a growth mindset, the sky's the limit!

55

You might have heard of the term "mindset" before, but do you know what it really means? Mindset refers to the way we think about ourselves, our abilities, and our potential. In other words, it's our attitude towards learning and growth. People usually have one of two mindsets: fixed mindset or growth mindset. We'll be discussing the differences between these two mindsets, and why having a growth mindset can make all the difference in your life.

To start off, let's define what each of these mindsets mean. A fixed mindset is when you believe that your qualities and abilities are predetermined and cannot be changed. You believe that your intelligence, talent, and personality are fixed traits that you were born with, and there is nothing you can do to improve them. On the other hand, a growth mindset is when you believe that your qualities and abilities can be developed through hard work and dedication. You see failures as opportunities to learn and you are always looking to improve yourself.

Now, let's look at some of the differences between these two mindsets. People with a fixed mindset tend to avoid challenges because they are afraid of failure. They believe that if they fail at something, it means they are not smart or talented enough. On the other hand, people with a growth mindset embrace challenges, even if they are difficult. They see challenges as opportunities to learn and grow.

Another difference between fixed and growth mindsets is how they view effort. People with a fixed mindset believe that effort is pointless because they think their abilities are predetermined. They don't see the value in hard work because they believe that success is based on natural talent. People with a growth mindset, on the other hand, believe that effort is essential for success. They see hard work as a way to improve and grow.

People with a fixed mindset also tend to give up easily when faced with obstacles. They believe that if they can't do something right away, it's not worth doing. They lack resilience and perseverance. People with a growth mindset, on the other hand, are more resilient and perseverant. They understand that learning takes time and effort, and they are willing to put in the work to achieve their goals.

Lastly, people with a fixed mindset tend to be jealous and envious of other people's successes. They believe that if someone else is successful, it means they are not. They see success as a zero-sum game. People with a growth mindset, on the other hand, are happy for other people's successes. They understand that everyone has their own path to success, and that someone else's success does not diminish their own potential.

Having a growth mindset can make all the difference in your life. It allows you to embrace challenges, see the value in hard work, be resilient and perseverant, and be happy for other people's successes. So, if you find yourself having a fixed mindset, don't worry, it's never too late to change. Start by embracing challenges, putting in the effort, and being happy for other people's successes. Remember, growth is not a destination, it's a journey, and the journey starts with your mindset.

Chapter 7
Psychology of the Mind

Welcome to a fascinating journey into the inner workings of the human mind. Our mind is the control center of our thoughts, emotions, and behavior. It shapes our personality, decisions, and interactions with the world around us. As college or university students, you must have come across several subjects that address the topic of psychology. The psychology of the mind is one of the most intriguing disciplines that scientists and scholars have dedicated their lives to understanding.

We will explore the basics of the psychology of the mind, its significance, its applications, and how it can help us in our daily lives. We will delve into the intricacies of the human mind, the different theories related to psychology, and the role of perception and emotions in psychology.

The psychology of the mind is a branch of psychology that focuses on the internal processes and associations that occur within our brains. It seeks to unravel the mysteries of how we perceive the world and how we respond to it. Through research, both experimental and clinical, psychologists study several aspects of the human mind, such as decision-making, cognitive processes, perception, motivation, and behavior.

One of the essential concepts related to the psychology of the mind is the unconscious mind. It is the part of our mind that operates behind the scenes, influencing our thoughts and behavior without us realizing it. It has been subject to several theories, such as Freud's psychoanalytic theory, that emphasized the role of unconsciousness in shaping our personality and behavior.

Today, researchers have built upon the foundations of Freud's theory and concluded that the unconscious mind plays an integral role in decision-making and behavior.

Another area of the psychology of the mind is the study of perception. Our perception shapes how we interpret the world around us. It involves the organization, interpretation, and integration of sensory information. Psychologists study perception to better understand how our mind processes information and forms a worldview. Perception also impacts our memory and affects how we remember specific experiences.

Emotions are also essential in psychology and play a significant role in shaping our behavior. Emotions are a complex mixture of physiological sensations and mental processes that occur in response to a stimulus such as an event or an object. They can be positive or negative and range from simple emotions like happiness and sadness to more complex emotions like jealousy and love.

Understanding emotions helps us better relate to others and can improve our relationships. For instance, by understanding different emotions' causes and effects, we can develop empathy and compassion towards others. It can also help us manage our emotions more effectively, leading to better mental and emotional health.

The psychology of the mind is a fascinating discipline that offers insights into the inner workings of the human mind. By understanding how our mind perceives the world, processes information, and forms a worldview, we can make better decisions and improve our interactions with others. As college or university students, you can benefit from learning about psychology and its applications in your academic and personal lives.

Keep in mind that understanding the psychology of the mind is a lifelong journey that requires dedication, curiosity, and an open mind. With this guide, you are one step closer to unlocking the mysteries of the mind, so get ready to go on a fun and insightful ride!

Chapter 8

Dominance: What it really means

When we think of dominance, we often associate it with aggressive behaviors and forceful personalities. However, dominance is not just about being loud and intimidating.

In social psychology, dominance refers to the influence one person has over another through subtle cues and body language. Dominance dynamics play a crucial role in our personal and professional relationships and understanding them can help us navigate social situations more effectively. We will explore what dominance entails, how it works and why it matters, particularly for college and university students.

Dominance is not limited to humans. Non-human animals also display dominance behaviors, and researchers have long studied the patterns of social hierarchy among them. Nevertheless, human dominance can be more complex and nuanced, as it often manifests in different forms across various settings. In social psychology, dominance frequently involves non-verbal expressions, such as eye contact, tone of voice, posture, and even fashion choices. These expressions may signal authority and confidence or submission and deference. Understanding the dominance cues that people send out can help us decode their intentions and respond accordingly.

Humans tend to respond to dominant cues unconsciously, as they have evolved to be hyper-vigilant to power dynamics.

For example, studies show that people tend to avoid eye contact with their superiors and make more eye contact with those lower in the social hierarchy. This behavior is thought to be a way of avoiding confrontation and sending signals of respect. People also tend to imitate the body posture and movements of dominant individuals, mirroring their behavior to show affiliation or to gain acceptance. By paying attention to these signals, we can gain insight into people's thinking and emotional states.

Dominance also plays a significant role in communication, particularly in groups. Dominant individuals often take charge of conversations, speaking more frequently and for longer periods than others. They may interrupt or talk over others, making it challenging for quieter members to get a word in. In group situations, it is important to be mindful of dominant individuals and not let them dominate the conversation. It is also essential to bring quieter people into the conversation, encouraging their participation and contributions.

Dominance can be helpful in certain circumstances, such as leading a team, delivering a speech, or negotiating a deal. However, dominance can also have negative effects, particularly when it becomes aggressive and intimidating. Aggressive dominance can undermine trust and limit collaboration, making it difficult to build relationships and get things done. Therefore, it is essential to balance dominance with warmth and empathy. Being supportive and understanding towards others can create a more positive and productive atmosphere and help build stronger relationships.

Dominance is a complex and multifaceted concept that plays an important role in social interactions. As college and university students, understanding dominance dynamics can help us navigate social situations more effectively, gain insight into others' emotions and motivations, and communicate and collaborate more effectively. Dominance is not just about being loud and aggressive; it can also show up in more subtle cues, such as non-verbal expressions. By paying attention to these signals and balancing dominance with warmth and empathy, we can build stronger relationships and succeed in our personal and professional lives.

65

If you're a college or university student, then you've probably heard the term 'dominance' in one of your classes or discussions. But what exactly does it mean? Is it just about exerting power over others, or is there more to it than meets the eye? We are going to explore the concept of dominance, its different interpretations, and how it relates to our daily lives.

According to the Merriam-Webster dictionary, dominance is "the fact or state of being dominant: such as, commanding, controlling, or prevailing over all others." In other words, it refers to a person, group, or entity that has power or authority over others and can make decisions or influence outcomes.

However, the meaning of dominance can be interpreted differently depending on the context. For example, in the animal kingdom, dominance is often associated with physical strength and aggression. The dominant animal asserts its control over the group and can reproduce, eat and access resources at will. In contrast, in human society, dominance can manifest itself in various forms, such as financial, social, intellectual, or emotional power.

Additionally, dominance can be both positive and negative. A positive form of dominance would be a leader who uses their influence to motivate and inspire their followers to achieve a common goal. They may have the authority to make decisions, but they listen to the opinions of others, and their actions benefit everyone. On the other hand, negative dominance would be a bully who intimidates, threatens, or harms others to get what they want. They may have a sense of power, but their actions harm others and lead to resentment and conflict.

Moreover, dominance can affect our daily lives in subtle ways that we may not even notice. For instance, when we scroll through social media, we're exposed to posts that are designed to catch our attention and keep us engaged. Companies use their dominance in the advertising industry to create a narrative that resonates with us and influences our behaviour. In politics, dominant parties or leaders can shape policies and laws that affect the lives of millions of people. Dominance can influence what we think, feel, and do, even if we're not aware of it.

Understanding the meaning of dominance is essential to navigate the complex social, economic, and political landscape that we live in. It's not just a matter of who has the most power or influence, but also how they use it and what impact it has on others. By being aware of different types of dominance and how they affect us, we can make informed decisions and challenge harmful or oppressive systems. So, let's continue exploring this fascinating concept and see how we can apply it to our lives.

Chapter 9

Dominating Business

Congratulations! You're finally in college, or maybe even nearing the end of it. Whichever point you're at, you're likely now thinking about your future, and more specifically, your career prospects. The world of business can be overwhelming, intimidating, and difficult to navigate. But don't worry, you've got this! Here are some tips on how to dominate the business world as a college or university student.:

Network, Network, Network

We've all heard it - it's not what you know, it's who you know. This may sound discouraging at first, but it's actually a fantastic opportunity. Use your college or university years to build relationships with professors, classmates, club members, and anyone else you come across. Attend career fairs, workshops, and events to meet industry professionals. You never know who may become a valuable connection in the future.

Gain Practical Experience

As much as theoretical knowledge is important, it's not enough on its own. Find internships, co-op programs, or part-time jobs in your field of interest. Not only will this give you practical experience and skills, but it will also allow you to build relationships with professionals in your desired industry.

Develop Your Personal Brand

What makes you unique? What sets you apart from others in your field? Consider developing a personal brand that showcases your strengths, values, and personality. This can include having a professional website or social media presence, creating a personal logo or tagline, or even just consistently showcasing your personal brand through your work.

Stay Informed

The business world is constantly evolving, and it's important to stay informed on industry trends, news, and best practices. Follow industry leaders, read business blogs, and attend conferences to stay up-to-date. This will not only deepen your knowledge and understanding of your field but may also provide you with valuable insights and connections.

Believe In Yourself

Most importantly, believe in yourself and your abilities. Don't let fear or self-doubt hold you back from pursuing your goals and dreams. Many successful business professionals started their journey as college or university students, just like you. Trust in your education, experiences, and skills, and you'll be well on your way to dominating the business world.

Becoming a successful business professional as a college or university student may seem daunting, but with the right approach, it's definitely achievable. Networking, gaining practical experience, developing your personal brand, staying informed, and believing in yourself are all essential steps to take on your journey. Don't be afraid to dream big and work hard. Who knows, you may just be the next big name in your industry!

The business world can be a cut-throat industry with fierce competition and high risk. Whether you're a college student, entrepreneur, or just looking to get ahead in your career, dominating the business world can be a daunting task. But don't worry, with the right mindset and strategies, you can put yourself in a position to succeed. Let's outline some tips and strategies that will help you become a dominant force in the business world.

Develop a Winner's Mindset

The first step to dominating the business world is developing a winner's mindset. This means believing in yourself, staying positive, and not being afraid to take risks. You need to be persistent, disciplined, and determined. Surround yourself with successful and like-minded individuals, and learn from their experiences. Read books, attend conferences, and take online courses to expand your knowledge and skills.

Network, Network, Network

Networking is a crucial part of building your business. Attend conferences, seminars, and other industry events to make contacts, share ideas, and learn from others. Join professional organizations, attend meetups and other networking events to establish your presence in the industry. Use social media to broaden your network, connect with influencers, and stay up-to-date with industry trends.

Embrace Technology

In today's business world, technological advancements have revolutionized the way we operate. Embrace technology and use it to your advantage. Learn how to use social media platforms, use online project management tools, and automate repetitive tasks. Stay up-to-date with the latest tech trends, and use them to improve your productivity, efficiency and stay ahead of the competition.

Focus on Innovation

Innovation is essential to dominate the business world. Don't be afraid to take risks and think creatively. Look for ways to revolutionize your industry, solve problems creatively, and offer better solutions than your competitors. Encourage your employees to be innovative, and provide them with the necessary resources and support.

Build a Strong Team

Building a strong team is vital for success in business. Hire talented individuals who share your vision, values and complement your skill set. Empower your team, delegate responsibility, and reward them for their accomplishments. Provide them with the necessary resources and support, and encourage them to take risks and be innovative.:

Becoming a dominant force in the business world requires a combination of hard work, determination, and the right strategies. Develop a winner's mindset, network, embrace technology, focus on innovation, and build a strong team to put yourself in a position to succeed. Be willing to take risks, learn from your failures, and don't be afraid to think outside the box. By implementing these strategies, you'll be on your way to dominating the business world.

Chapter 10
Dominating Finances

Money matters! It can be a constant source of stress or an avenue to financial freedom. If you're a college student or an entrepreneur, you may feel overwhelmed with managing your finances. It can be tough, but it's definitely not impossible. The biggest obstacle is not having enough knowledge about how to dominate your finances. Let's address that lack of knowledge by providing information and practical tips on how to take control of your finances, reduce financial stress, and increase financial security.

Set a Budget

The first step to dominating your finances is to set a budget. A budget is a plan for how you will spend the money you have. It forces you to consider your financial priorities and allocate your resources accordingly. You can use a spreadsheet or a budgeting app to create your budget. Make sure to include all your sources of income and all your expenses. Try to reduce your expenses as much as possible, while still making sure you can cover all your basic needs.

Build an Emergency Fund

An emergency fund is money that you set aside for unexpected expenses, such as medical bills or car repairs. It's important to have an emergency fund because it can prevent you from going into debt or relying on credit cards. Ideally, your emergency fund should be able to cover at least three to six months of living expenses. If you're a college student or an entrepreneur, it may be tough to save up that amount of money. Start small; even saving $10 or $20 a week can add up over time.

Avoid High-Interest Debt

Credit cards and payday loans may seem like easy ways to get money, but they often come with high interest rates. High-interest debt can quickly spiral out of control and leave you drowning in debt. Instead of relying on credit cards or loans, try to live within your means. If you can't afford something right now, save up for it or find a cheaper alternative. If you already have high-interest debt, focus on paying it off as soon as possible.

Invest in Your Future

Investing is a great way to grow your wealth over time. If you're a college student or an entrepreneur, you may not have a lot of money to invest right now. However, starting to invest early can have a huge impact on your future wealth. You can start small by investing in a low-cost index fund. As you earn more income, you can increase your investment contributions.

Take Advantage of Financial Resources

Don't forget to take advantage of financial resources that are available to you. If you're a college student, your school may offer financial counseling or workshops. If you're an entrepreneur, there may be free resources or mentorship programs in your area. Do your research and take advantage of any resources that can help you improve your financial situation.

:

Dominating your finances is not an easy feat, but it's definitely worth the effort. By setting a budget, building an emergency fund, avoiding high-interest debt, investing in your future, and taking advantage of financial resources, you can take control of your finances and achieve financial security. Remember, it's never too early or too late to start taking steps towards financial freedom. So, take action today, and start dominating your finances!

Being young and carefree is one of the most exhilarating phases of life. However, it's also the time when most people make financial mistakes that can haunt them for a long time. The importance of money management in your early years cannot be overstated. It sets the tone for your financial future, and it's never too early or too late to start. So, whether you're a college student with a part-time job or an aspiring entrepreneur, you need to take your finances seriously. Let's take a look at why money management is crucial in your early years.:

.Debt Repayment:

The first and foremost importance of money management is debt repayment. Many students ignore their education loans, credit card bills, and other debts, thinking that they'll deal with it later. But this ignorance can lead to serious financial consequences, such as being stuck in debt for years or even defaulting on payments. It's essential to create a budget that allows you to balance your expenses and debt repayment. The earlier you start repaying your debts, the better it is.

Building an Emergency Fund:

Emergencies can happen anytime, and it's crucial to be prepared. Building an emergency fund is one of the essential aspects of money management. You never know when you might need the extra cash, whether it's a medical emergency or a job loss. A common rule of thumb is to save at least three to six months' worth of expenses. It may seem overwhelming, but it's feasible with budgeting and saving skills.

Saving for Long-term Goals:

It's easy to get caught up in the moment and forget about the future. However, it's critical to set long-term financial goals and be committed to them. Whether it's saving for a down payment on a house or a retirement fund, your early years are the best time to start saving. By setting long-term goals, you can create a financial plan that will help you achieve your desired outcome without stress.

Investment Opportunities:

Investing can feel daunting, especially when you're young and inexperienced. However, it's crucial to learn about the different investment opportunities available to you. Investing in stocks, mutual funds, and real estate can help you build your wealth over time. With the right knowledge, you can make informed investment decisions that will significantly benefit your financial future.

Lifestyle Choices:

Your lifestyle choices can significantly impact your finances. It's essential to distinguish between your needs and wants and to prioritize your expenses. Living below your means can help you save more money and avoid unnecessary debt. Additionally, being mindful of your spending can help you develop good money habits that will benefit you throughout your life.

:

The importance of money management in your early years cannot be overstated. It's crucial to establish good financial habits that set the foundation for a secure financial future. By incorporating debt repayment, emergency funds, long-term goals, investment opportunities, and lifestyle choices into your money management strategy, you can position yourself for success. Remember, it's never too early or too late to start managing your finances better. Plan wisely and make a better financial future for yourself!

There's no doubt that money plays a big role in our lives, whether we like it or not. It's the fuel that keeps us going, the resource that enables us to pursue our dreams and achieve our goals. But for many of us, money is also a source of stress and anxiety, something that we struggle to manage or feel guilty about. What sets the winners apart is their money mindset, a set of beliefs and attitudes that shape their relationship with money and empower them to succeed. Let's explore what the winner's money mindset looks like, how to develop it, and why it matters.

Focus on growth, not scarcity

One of the hallmarks of the winner's money mindset is a focus on growth and abundance, rather than scarcity and lack. Instead of thinking that there's only a limited amount of money available and fearing that they won't get their share, winners believe that there's always more to be earned and created. They see money as a tool that can be leveraged for positive change and growth, both for themselves and others. This mindset allows them to adopt a proactive, entrepreneurial, and creative approach to money, taking risks and seeking out opportunities rather than playing it safe.

Embrace their value and worth

Another key feature of the winner's money mindset is a strong sense of self-worth and value. Winners know that their skills, talents, and contributions are valuable and in demand, and they're not afraid to ask for fair compensation and negotiate on their behalf. They don't settle for less than they deserve or let others dictate their worth. This confidence and assertiveness can be challenging to develop, especially if you've been conditioned to believe that money is a taboo subject or that asking for more is rude or greedy. But with practice and mindset shifts, you can learn to embrace your value and communicate it effectively.

Think long-term and strategic

Winners don't just think about money in the short term, as a means to an end. They take a long-term, strategic approach to money that involves setting goals, tracking progress, and making informed decisions. They understand the power of compound interest, investing, and diversification, and they prioritize saving and building wealth over instant gratification. This mindset helps them avoid impulsive purchases, debt, and financial instability, and enables them to create sustainable, scalable, and impactful ventures and businesses. To cultivate this mindset, start by defining your financial goals, creating a budget and investing plan, and educating yourself on personal finance and entrepreneurship.

Use money as a tool for good

Winners see money as a tool for good, not just for themselves but also for their communities and society as a whole. They're conscious of the impact that their financial decisions and behaviors have on the environment, social justice, and ethical values, and they seek to align their values with their actions. They give back to the causes they care about, support local businesses and entrepreneurs, and invest in socially responsible funds and companies. This mindset not only enables them to make a positive contribution to the world but also enhances their reputation, network, and legacy.

:

Developing a winner's money mindset is not an easy or overnight process, but it's a worthwhile one that can transform your relationship with money and your life. By adopting a growth-oriented, self-affirming, long-term, and values-driven approach to money, you'll be able to unlock your full potential, create more opportunities, and make a positive impact on the world. Whether you're a college student, an aspiring entrepreneur, or anyone who wants to improve their financial well-being, cultivating a winner's money mindset is a key step towards success. So go ahead, raise your financial game, and become a true winner.

Chapter 11
Colorization in Business

They say that colors speak louder than words and in the world of business, this rings especially true. Color is an art form that can make or break your brand, leaving a lasting impression on your customers. The use of color can set the tone for your business and even change the way people perceive it. From the bright green of Starbucks to the vibrant red of Coca-Cola, colours are what make businesses come alive. We will explore the power of color in business, and how you can use it to enhance your brand's image.

Understanding the psychology of color

The psychology of color is a complex field but can be summarised into four main categories: warm colors, cool colors, neutral colours and muted colors. Warm colors such as red, orange and yellow are energising and evoke feelings of passion and warmth. Cool colors like blue, green and purple are more calming and can evoke feelings of trust and reliability. Neutral colors like black, white and grey, on the other hand, are more professional and can be used to convey a sense of luxury. Muted colors like pastel shades, may not be as powerful on their own but can be used to enhance other colors.

Color in branding

Color is an essential part of branding, and it's vital to choose the right colours for your brand. Colors can express personality, convey emotions and evoke memories. For example, an eco-friendly business may choose green to represent their brand while a coffee shop may choose a warm brown. It's important to keep in mind, however, the cultural relevance of colors. For example, in Western cultures, white is associated with purity, while in Asian cultures, it is associated with mourning. Therefore, it's critical to research the cultural influences of colors before finalising your brand's colours.

Color in marketing

Color is a powerful marketing tool that can grab attention and draw in customers. It can even increase purchase intent by up to 80%. It's important to use colors strategically in marketing campaigns. For example, a clearance sale campaign may use bright red to catch a shopper's attention while a fitness brand may use black to convey strength and determination. Through the use of color, brands can evoke emotions, convey a message and differentiate themselves from their competitors.

Using color in websites

In today's digital age, having a visually appealing website has become more critical than ever before. Color can impact the way people view your website and how long they stay on it. A study found that using colors can increase brand recognition by up to 80%. By using colors strategically, businesses can increase website conversions, engagement and overall customer satisfaction.

Colors to Avoid

While there's no right or wrong colour in business, there are some colors that businesses should avoid. Using too much red can be seen as aggressive and overwhelming, while too much black can be seen as negative. Another colors to avoid is yellow, which can be challenging to read and cause eye strain over time. It's essential to use these colors sparingly or not to use them at all to maintain a positive brand image.

Color is a critical aspect of business and can significantly impact the way people perceive your brand. By understanding the psychology of color, businesses can use it to convey emotions, grab attention and differentiate themselves from competitors. When choosing colors for your brand, make sure to research cultural relevance and use them strategically in your marketing campaigns. Remember that colors speak profusely, so make sure to choose the right ones to represent your brand's vision and personality. Start by gathering inspiration, experimenting and exploring the colours that best represent your brand and audience. Happy coloring!

83

One of the great things about being an entrepreneur is that your success is not dependent on your background or the color of your skin. That being said, the harsh reality is that being a person of color in the business world has its own set of challenges. Discrimination and bias are still rampant, and it can often feel like you're fighting an uphill battle.

However, this should not deter you from pursuing your dreams. With the right mindset and support, you can overcome these difficulties and thrive in the business world. Let's explore some of the challenges that people of color face in the business world and offer some tips on how to navigate them.

Bias and discrimination: Unfortunately, bias and discrimination are still prevalent in many industries, and people of color often face these challenges. Whether it's being passed over for promotions or not being taken seriously in meetings, these experiences can be frustrating and demoralizing.

One way to navigate these challenges is to be confident and assertive. Don't be afraid to speak up and assert your ideas, even if they're different from what others in the room are saying. Additionally, seek out mentors and allies who can support you and offer advice on how to navigate these challenges.

Lack of representation: People of color are often underrepresented in leadership positions and in the business world as a whole. This lack of representation can make it difficult to find mentors, networks, and role models.

To navigate this challenge, it's essential to seek out communities and organizations that offer support and representation for people of color. Attend events and conferences that are geared towards underrepresented communities in your industry, join professional organizations, and seek out mentors who share your background and experiences.

Imposter syndrome: Imposter syndrome is something that many entrepreneurs and business leaders struggle with, but it can be especially challenging for people of color. When you're constantly being told that you don't belong or that you're not good enough, it can be easy to internalize these messages and doubt your abilities.

To overcome imposter syndrome, surround yourself with people who believe in you and will support you when you're feeling down. Seek out mentors who can offer guidance and advice on how to navigate the business world. Additionally, take time to celebrate your wins and acknowledge your successes. You've worked hard to get where you are, and you deserve to feel proud of your accomplishments.

Microaggressions: Microaggressions are subtle, often unintentional comments or actions that can be hurtful or dismissive. People of color often experience these in the business world, whether it's being asked where they're "really" from or being complimented on their English skills.

To navigate microaggressions, it's essential to be assertive and to speak up when they occur. Don't be afraid to call people out on their behavior and explain why their actions or comments are hurtful. Additionally, seek out communities and organizations that offer support and validation for people of color. Being able to talk to others who have had similar experiences can be incredibly helpful.:

Navigating the business world as a person of color can be challenging, but it's important to remember that your background and experiences don't define your success. With the right mindset and support, you can overcome these challenges and achieve your goals. Seek out mentors and allies, surround yourself with supportive communities, and don't be afraid to speak up and assert your ideas. Your unique perspective and experiences are valuable, and the business world needs more entrepreneurs and leaders like you.

Chapter 12

Colorization in Relationships

Love has always been perceived to be colorblind, does it really matter? The color of love doesn't define the strength of a relationship or its longevity. However, a relationship's foundation can be built on compatibility, common interests, mutual respect, and pride in one's heritage. We will explore the impact of colorisation in relationships, how it affects its dynamics, the conversations around the topic, and the role you can play in creating a more inclusive narrative.

The discussion of colorisation in relationships has been an ongoing conversation in the world for centuries. The intersectionality of skin color, culture, religion, and social class have contributed to social constructs that create divides in social and romantic relationships. Regardless of skin color, socio-economic status, or religion, relationships need to be able to thrive in a space of mutual respect, honesty, and care. However, acknowledgement of one's skin color and its cultural implications should not be overlooked. For example, in a culture (or race) that upholds certain practices and values, it's essential to recognize such values when building a relationship with someone who is from a different culture (or race). It doesn't mean that the relationship will be doomed to fail; rather, acknowledging each other's cultural differences can go a long way to strengthen the bond between both parties.

Research shows that interpersonal relationships between people from different races or ethnic backgrounds have their own unique challenges. Such relationships tend to attract extra attention from external forces that can play either positively or negatively. In some cases, family and friends from different cultural backgrounds may have different views or may be narrow-minded when it comes to the concept of colorisation in relationships. This can cause a strain on the relationship and can lead to disapproval from certain external forces. Prejudice, lack of understanding of someone's culture, or refusal to acknowledge the cultural importance in relationships can be detrimental to the success of an interracial or intercultural relationship.

Having open conversations about colorisation in relationships can help people to understand and embrace different cultures. Acknowledging the cultural and racial differences can also provide an opportunity to learn more about one's own culture while getting to know another. This open dialogue also opens up the space for both parties to build further trust, acceptance and understanding.

Relationships aren't only built on love and attraction. Respect and acceptance are also fundamental. Integration of different cultures and races in relationships can be a positive outcome. Genuine respect, pride and acceptance of one's heritage can go a long way in building a strong bond between people from different cultures. In a world where diversity is celebrated, it's essential to embrace one's uniqueness and include each other's cultural beliefs. We are all human beings with unique stories and backgrounds that deserve to be respected, honour, and celebrated.

Colorisation in relationships is an essential aspect to consider and acknowledge. While love is colorblind, respecting and honouring each other's cultural and racial differences can help to strengthen and build a more inclusive society. It's essential to have open and honest conversations to lead to respect, trust, and mutual understanding. Together we can celebrate and embrace our diversity while building a more accepting and loving world.

They say love knows no boundaries, and in today's increasingly globalized world, mixed culture and interracial relationships have become less of a rarity. In fact, it is estimated that over 10% of marriages in the United States are between partners of different races or ethnicities. However, navigating the complexities of a relationship where two individuals have different cultures, languages, and belief systems can be tough without open communication. Let's discuss why open communication is critical in mixed culture relationships and how it can enhance your relationship and bond with your partner.

Acknowledge Cultural Differences

When we enter into a mixed culture relationship, it is essential to acknowledge our cultural differences. What may seem like a harmless gesture in one culture can be interpreted negatively in another, leading to misunderstandings, confusion, and even conflict. Therefore, acknowledging our cultural differences, and approaching them with an open mind and a willingness to learn from each other, is crucial.

Language Barriers

Language barriers can be a significant obstacle in mixed culture relationships, but they don't have to be. If your partner's language is different from yours, making an effort to learn their language shows that you value their culture and want to communicate with them more effectively. Both partners need to be patient and make an effort to communicate clearly with one another.

Understanding Each Other's Values

In any relationship, knowing your partner's values is vital, and this is particularly crucial in mixed culture relationships. Different cultures have various values, and we must acknowledge and appreciate them. Open communication allows for a better understanding of each other's values, which can strengthen the relationship's bond. It is essential to understand that your partner's values may differ from your own, and that is okay.

Dealing with Agreements and Disagreements

Every relationship experiences conflicts, and for mixed culture relationships, these conflicts can be magnified due to communication barriers and cultural misunderstandings. Open communication can help in dealing with these disagreements as it provides a means of expressing concerns and ideas freely, without judgment or criticism. Listening to each other's opinions and finding common ground may require compromise, but it may lead to a stronger and healthier relationship.

Be Respectful

Respect is a universal value that everyone needs to cultivate in a relationship, not only in mixed culture relationships. Demonstrating respect for your partner's perspective, beliefs, and decisions creates a strong foundation of trust and understanding. It's okay to disagree, but respecting each other's opinions is paramount to the success of the relationship.

:

While mixed culture relationships can be rich and fulfilling, they come with their unique set of challenges. Open communication is the key to navigating these challenges and building a strong and healthy relationship. By understanding each other's culture, acknowledging and respecting differences, understanding values, and communicating honestly, couples can find common ground and enjoy a fulfilling relationship. With a willingness to learn and listen, anything is possible in a mixed culture relationship.

As a black person in the business world, it can be difficult to navigate a system that was not necessarily designed with us in mind. But fear not! There are plenty of examples of successful black entrepreneurs and professionals who have made their mark in the business world. So how can you follow in their footsteps? Here are some tips on how to be black and dominate the business world.

Know your worth and believe in yourself

One of the biggest obstacles that black professionals and entrepreneurs face is imposter syndrome. We often feel like we don't belong or that our achievements are not truly deserved. But it's important to remember that you have worked hard to get where you are, and you have earned your place in the business world. Don't be afraid to seize opportunities and take risks – believe in yourself and your abilities.

Build a strong network

Networking is crucial in any industry, but it can be especially important for black professionals who may not have the same access to opportunities as their white counterparts. Make connections with other black professionals and entrepreneurs, attend events and conferences, and reach out to mentors who can help guide you in your career. Your network can open doors and provide support when you need it most.

Educate yourself on business and finance

Knowledge is power, and in the business world, it can mean the difference between success and failure. Take the time to learn about finance, marketing, and management – whether through formal education or self-study. This will not only increase your confidence, but also make you a more valuable asset to any company or organization you work for.

Stay true to your identity and values

Being black is not a disadvantage in the business world – in fact, it can be a strength. As a black professional, you bring a unique perspective and set of experiences that can be valuable in any industry. Don't feel like you need to assimilate or conform to a certain standard of professionalism. Embrace your identity and values and use them to differentiate yourself from the competition.

Pay it forward

Finally, as you make your way in the business world, don't forget to pay it forward. Mentor other black professionals and entrepreneurs, give back to your community, and use your success to create opportunities for others. Not only will this help build a stronger network and community, but it will also contribute to a more diverse and equitable business world for future generations.

So, there you have it – some tips on how to be black and dominate the business world. Remember to believe in yourself, build a strong network, educate yourself, stay true to your identity and values, and pay it forward. With hard work, dedication, and a little bit of luck, there's no reason why you can't succeed in the business world as a black professional or entrepreneur. Good luck!

Chapter 13
Women Who Run The World

Gone are the days when women were relegated to the background, confined to traditional roles and treated as second-class citizens. Today, more and more women are taking the world by storm, proving that they can do anything that men can, and sometimes even better. From politics to business, entertainment and beyond, women have made significant strides in different fields and continue to inspire people with their success stories.

Let us highlight some women who run the world, breaking barriers and shattering stereotypes along the way. If you're a college or university student, or an entrepreneur looking for inspiration, look no further.

Politics

Women have always been underrepresented in politics, but now, more and more are stepping up to the challenge and proving that they've got what it takes to lead. For instance, Kamala Harris, the first female, Black, and South Asian Vice President in the history of the United States, made history with her election in 2020. Jacinda Ardern, the current Prime Minister of New Zealand, is another inspiring political leader who has gained worldwide recognition for her leadership during the COVID-19 pandemic.

Business

For years, the business world was seen as a man's domain, but that's rapidly changing as women claim their place in the corporate world. From Mary Barra, the CEO of General

Motors, to Ginni Rometty, the Executive Chairman of IBM, and even Oprah Winfrey, our favorite talk show host and media mogul, women are proving their worth in the world of business.

Entertainment

When it comes to entertainment, women have been dominating the scene for years, from Beyoncé to Lady Gaga, to Cardi B. But it's not just in music that women are making waves. Women actors, directors, and writers like Viola Davis, Chloé Zhao, Shonda Rhimes, and Issa Rae are also paving the way for others and showing that women can excel in any field.

Sports

For years, people have thought of sports as a predominantly male field. Still, women are showing that they can excel in sports just as well as men can. Serena Williams, the tennis superstar, has been making history and breaking records since she first picked up a racket. Similarly, women's soccer teams like the US Women's National Team and the Lyon Olympique emerged as champions at the 2019 Women's World Cup, proving that women can play soccer just as well as men.

Technology

In the field of technology, we have women like Sheryl Sandberg, the COO of Facebook, and Susan Wojcicki, the CEO of YouTube, making waves and smashing barriers. These women have been instrumental in shaping the tech industry and inspire others to pursue careers in the field.

These inspiring women who run the world have shown you that anything is possible if you put your mind to it. Whether you're a college or university student or an entrepreneur, you can achieve your goals and break barriers, just like these women did. It's time to shatter stereotypes and push the boundaries, so let's get inspired and make history!

Being a leader is tough work. You are responsible for setting an example for your followers, helping them achieve their goals, and ensuring that your team is working towards the greater good. If you want to make a difference in the world and be a successful entrepreneur, you need to develop certain traits that will help you become a good leader. Here are the top 5 traits of a good leader.

Vision

One of the most important traits of a good leader is having a clear vision. A leader with a vision knows where they want to take their team or organization and is fully dedicated to achieving it. They are able to articulate their vision in a way that inspires their followers and attracts the necessary resources to make it a reality. Without vision, a leader will be directionless, and their followers will struggle to understand where they are going.

Communication

Good communication skills are essential for any leader. Being able to convey your ideas clearly and effectively ensures that your followers know what is expected of them. Additionally, good communication skills help build relationships with your followers, which is crucial for creating a positive work environment. As a leader, you need to be an effective listener, and you need to be able to give feedback constructively.

Adaptability

The world is constantly changing, and as a leader, you need to be able to adapt to these changes. Being adaptable means being able to pivot when necessary and being open to new ideas and ways of doing things. Additionally, good leaders are able to learn from their mistakes and take corrective action when needed. Being rigid and refusing to adapt can hinder your organization's growth and lead to missed opportunities.

Empathy

Empathy is an important trait for leaders to have because it allows them to connect with their followers on a personal level. Empathetic leaders recognize their followers' feelings, and they are able to respond appropriately. Empathy also helps leaders make better decisions and create more inclusive work environments, where everyone feels valued and heard.

Delegation

A good leader knows that they cannot do everything themselves. Delegation is an essential skill for any leader because it allows them to focus on their core responsibilities while trusting their followers to handle other tasks. Delegation also helps develop your followers' skills, which can lead to increased productivity and job satisfaction. As a leader, it is important to delegate tasks that are appropriate for your followers' skill sets and to provide them with the necessary resources and support.

Being a leader is not easy, but developing these five traits can help you stand out from the crowd and become a successful entrepreneur. Remember, developing your leadership skills is an ongoing process, and it takes time and effort to cultivate these traits. As you continue to grow as a leader, always keep in mind the importance of vision, communication, adaptability, empathy, and delegation. With these traits in your toolkit, you will be able to effectively lead your team or organization towards success. Good luck!

Gone are the days when leaders were exclusively male. Women have been breaking barriers and excelling in various fields, including politics, business, academia, and other industries. But what makes women good leaders? Is it just a matter of gender, or are there other factors at play? Let's examine the traits of successful female leaders and how they excel in their roles.

Empathy - Women tend to be more empathetic than men, which is a valuable trait for leaders. Empathy allows leaders to understand their team's needs and concerns and to communicate with them effectively. By putting themselves in their team's shoes, women can gain valuable insights and make strategic decisions.

Collaboration - Many successful women leaders have a collaborative management style, which fosters creativity and innovation. Instead of controlling or micromanaging, they empower their team members to contribute ideas and solutions. This approach leads to more diverse and effective solutions to problems.

Resilience - Women in leadership roles often face more challenges and criticism than their male counterparts. However, they also tend to be resilient and adaptable, which enables them to overcome obstacles and maintain their leadership positions. Resilience is a critical factor in success, and women leaders possess this quality in spades.

Communication - Women are known for their excellent communication skills, which is a valuable trait in leadership roles. Clear, concise, and persuasive communication is essential for effective leadership, and women do it with ease. They can effectively convey their vision, motivate their team members, and build strong relationships with stakeholders.

Vision - Women leaders are known for having a clear vision for the future and their organizations. They are goal-oriented and determined to achieve their objectives. Having a clear vision is essential for leadership, as it provides direction and purpose for the team.

Women are excellent leaders for many reasons, including their empathy, collaboration, resilience, communication, and vision. As more women assume leadership roles, we are seeing positive changes in many industries and organizations. It is essential to continue to support and encourage women to pursue leadership positions and contribute to the growth and success of their communities. So, take inspiration from these leading ladies and strive to cultivate these traits in yourself to become a great leader.

Epilogue

Too often we forget our greatness, and our place in society. Life is meant to be enjoyed by all people, regardless or race, color or religion.

Dominance is a reminder that we can dominate, no matter who we are. We have the capabilities to achieve all that we desire in life; but not by ourselves. We need each other to strengthen us and remind us of our greatness on days we fall short.

As the popular saying goes, "no man is an island, no man stands alone." In order to achieve greatness, we need each other, in the right quantities, at the right time.

We have the power to dominate in areas we are not aware of, if only we try.

What is holding you back? You!

How long will you remain in the shadows of fear, neglect, guilt, and self-doubt?

It is time to dominate!

Works Cited

Allure. (2017). Retrieved from What Is 'Black Girl Magic'? : https://www.allure.com/story/what-is-black-girl-magic

Byrdie. (2018). *What Is Black Girl Magic? Here's the Full History. Retrieved from* . Retrieved from https://www.byrdie.com/what-is-black-girl-magic

Cosby, H. (2016). Retrieved from A Definition of Black Girl Magic: Celebrating Our Supernatural Living. Retrieved from : http://hellobeautiful.com/playlist/black-girl-magic-definition/

Essence. (2020). Retrieved from What Is Black Girl Magic? : https://www.essence.com/lifestyle/what-is-black-girl-magic

Gurira, D. (2017). Retrieved from How Black Women Can Embrace Their Power - PEN World Voices – The New School. : https://www.newschool.edu/public-engagement/danai-gurira-black-women-power/

Gurira, D. (2017). Retrieved from How Black Women Can Embrace Their Power - PEN World Voices – The New School. : https://www.newschool.edu/public-engagement/danai-gurira-black-women/

Huffington Post. (2017). Retrieved from Black Girl Magic: The Phenomenon Celebrating Our Achievements. Retrieved from: https://www.huffpost.com/entry/black-girl-magic_n_59d8da22e4b03e6857a6cf13

King, E. (2016). Retrieved from Black Girl Magic: The Movement Celebrating the Power and Beauty of Black Women Everywhere.: https://www.essence.com/lifestyle/what-is-black-girl-magic

Lodge, A. R. (2019). Retrieved from What Is Black Girl Magic? : https://www.youtube.com/watch?v=ymxKwzy7o8U&t=113s

Michaela, B. (2016). Retrieved from The Power Of 'Black Girl Magic': What It Is And Why We Need It Now: https://www.huffpost.com/entry/black-girl-magic_b_58ea05c3e4b0d9b5a02ca1ad?guccounter=1&guce_referrer=aHR0cHM6Ly93d3cuZ29vZ2xlLmNvbS88&guce_referrer_s

News, C. (2016). Retrieved from The Power of Black Women: 'Black Girl Magic': https://www.cbsnews.com/news/black-girl-magic-3/

Olufemi, T. (2018). *What Is Black Girl Magic? A Look at the Meaning Behind the Slogan.* Retrieved from https://www.teenvogue.com/story/what-is-black-girl-magic

Oulfemi, T. (2018). *What Is Black Girl Magic? A Look at the Meaning Behind the Slogan.* . Retrieved from https://www.teenvogue.com/story/what-is-black-girl-magic

Program, A. A. (2017). Retrieved from Black Girl Magic: The Power of Female Empowerment. Retrieved from : https://aas.stanford.edu/black-girl-magic

Vogue, T. (2020). Retrieved from Black Girl Magic: Why It Matters and How to Celebrate It: https://www.teenvogue.com/story/what-is-black-girl-magic

105

About the Author

Dr. Kalesha L. Henlon is an Educator and Mindset Relationship Coach. Dr. Henlon aims to provide a platform that allows others to realise their individual importance in society; not being shackled by societal norms, but constantly breaking barriers.

This book outlines the importance of self-love and self-care as a black person, striving to become the best version of themselves.

Black Entrepreneurs need to understand the importance of their existence and embrace it. There are no coincidences in life, everything happens for a reason – the way it should.

If you are Black – embrace it!

If you are White – embrace it!

If you are Asian – embrace it!

If you are Mixed – embrace it!

Regardless of your circumstances, embrace who you are and let your light shine bright!